I Am Brave Like David...
Right?

Elle Stahlhut Roetzel unpacks the power of God's Word through the backdrop of a boy named David. Although plagued by fear, you'll see a soul set free. Adults and kids alike will grow in their faith as they experience the Word of God in a fresh way. Read with an open heart. This book will challenge you and change you in the process.

—Kary Oberbrunner, Author of ELIXIR Project, Day Job to Dream Job, The Deeper Path, and Your Secret Name

I Am Brave Like David...
Right?

Elle Stahlhut Roetzel

Illustrations by Diane Schleyhahn

DEDICATION

This book is dedicated to my children, Ben, Daniel and Lydia. May they continue to know and experience the power of God's love for them which is greater than that which comes against them.

I also want to dedicate this book to my Iowa Mom's Prayer Group. As we came together and shared our struggles and victories we saw God move powerfully in the lives of our children and neighborhood. This book was inspired by one of those prayer times as a mom shared about her son's struggle with fear. God gave me this vision of David to pray over her son. The Lord then told me that the vision He gave me to pray was a book. This is the book that you hold in your hands. May the Lord be glorified for releasing this young boy from his fears.

Foreword

As a young girl, I loved the Word of God and read it from cover to cover several times. Though I was saved and was in the Word, I did not give all of who I was to the Lord, nor did I trust Him to help me daily. It wasn't until my world came crashing down around me that I knew I needed to trust something that was solid and true. It is then that I recommitted my life to the Lord and began my journey of experiencing His Word as my truth.

It is my deepest desire for children and adults to know that God is a good God and that His truth is greater than our emotions and greater than the things that come against us in this world. As He has healed me from the hurts in my soul and led me through the storms of this world I have found Him faithful and true. He is the solid foundation that I was always longing for. His love is the love that I had always desired.

It is my prayer that as you and your children read this book, you will be stirred by the Holy Spirit to stand on the Word of God over and above what you are feeling, what the world may be telling you, or even what those around you are telling you to do. Blessings upon blessings begin to flow into our lives when we live out of the truth of Jesus and His Word.

Elle Stahlhut Roetzel

Hi my name is David. I live with my dad, mom, and big sister. I spend most of my time going to school. When I am not in school I love to play basketball, baseball, football, and kickball with my friends in the neighborhood. When I go to bed at night I am exhausted, but my mom and dad read me bedtime stories anyway. They say it helps me learn and become smart.

Like I said, I am usually tired when I finally get to bed but when mom or dad read me my favorite bedtime story about David, I am wide awake. I was named after David in the Bible. He was a shepherd boy who became King.

It's kind of cool that mom and dad named me after my favorite Bible person. So, I must be just like David, right?

David is strong. SO AM I.

PSALM 138:3 Thank you! Everything in me says "Thank you!" Angels listen as I sing my thanks. I kneel in worship facing your holy temple and say it again: "Thank you!" Thank you for your love, thank you for your faithfulness; most holy is your name, most holy is your Word. The moment I called out, you stepped in; you made my life large with strength."

David is brave. SO AM I.

1 SAMUEL 17:32 "Master," said David, "don't give up hope. I'm ready to go and fight this Philistine."

David loved to worship God. SO DO I

PSALM 103:1 "O my soul, bless GOD. From head to toe, I'll bless his holy name!"

WAS David ever afraid? AM I?

David was so brave. David was the only one who went to stand against the giant named Goliath. David didn't take a sword. David didn't ask anyone else to come with him. David just took his slingshot. Even when he felt afraid, he knew that he could trust God and God would deliver him.

1 SAMUEL 17:38-40 "Then David took his shepherd's staff, selected five smooth stones from the brook, and put them in the pocket of his shepherd's pack, and with his sling in his hand, he approached Goliath."

At night, when my mom reads me the story about David, I think about fighting bears and lions. I stand up strong on my bed and grab them by their heads and fling them over.

So, I'm brave like David too, right?

1 SAMUEL 17:34-37 "David said, "I've been a shepherd, tending sheep for my father. Whenever a lion or bear came and took a lamb from the flock, I'd go after it, knock it down, and rescue the lamb. If it turned on me, I'd grab it by the throat, wring its neck, and kill it. Lion or bear, it made no difference—I killed it."

Well.... maybe, I'm not. When there is a thunderstorm outside, and the sky lights up from the lightening blast, and the roar of thunder fills my ears, I want to hide under my bed!! I forget all about being brave.

My mom tells me to remember the Bible verses that I have hidden in my heart. She tells me to always remember that God is with me, so I never have to be afraid.

JOSHUA 1:9 "Haven't I commanded you? Strength! Courage! Don't be timid; don't get discouraged. GOD, your God, is with you every step you take."

I do a really good job remembering my Bible verses when I am practicing them for Sunday School. BUT when there is a storm outside or I have to go down to my dark basement all by myself, I have a hard time remembering anything except that I'm afraid.

PSALM 119:16 "I ponder every morsel of wisdom from you, I attentively watch how you've done it. I relish everything you've told me of life, I won't forget a word of it."

Holy Bible

My mom wanted to help me so she bought me a slingshot, just like David had in the Bible! WOW.

She said that the Word of God is strong and powerful and that fear runs from it!

Mom said that just like the slingshot flung the stone and knocked down Goliath the giant, I can speak my Bible verses from my heart and they will knock down fear.

1 SAMUEL 17:49-50 "That's how David beat the Philistine—with a sling and a stone. He hit him and killed him. No sword for David!"

I practiced with my dad all that night to make sure I had good aim. He set up my stuffed animals around the basement so that I could pretend to kill bears and lions. I didn't always hit the target but Dad told me that I didn't have to have the best aim because Jesus would make sure it hit the target.

WOW! Jesus would do that for me!!

ROMANS 8:34 "Do you think anyone is going to be able to drive a wedge between us and Christ's love for us? There is no way! Not trouble, not hard times, not hatred, not hunger, not homelessness, not bullying threats, not backstabbing, not even the worst sins listed in Scripture."

David knew his God. My mom said that I know my God too. I learn about Him through my Bible verses. Now it was time to stand strong on their truth, just like Mom had said.

That night when I went to sleep, all I could think about was what I had learned. It was like every Bible verse I had ever known went racing through my mind.

Be strong and
courageous ...
Joshua 1:9

When I got up the next morning, I felt strong, courageous, and ready for anything.

I went to school tall and strong as I rode my bike. I pretended that there were bears and lions all around me, but I made it through. I didn't even have to pull out the slingshot that was in my backpack. I was strong.

JOSHUA 10:25 "Joshua told them, "Don't hold back. Don't be timid. Be strong! Be confident! This is what God will do to all your enemies when you fight them.""

On the way home from school that night I took the slingshot out of my backpack and put it in my back pocket. I was going to be ready no matter how many bears and lions I found on my way home!

As I rode a few blocks from school I noticed that there were dark clouds just behind me. My first thought was, "Oh No! Not a storm! I'm scared of storms!" I felt the slingshot pressing in on me from my back pocket. "That's right," I thought, "I have everything I need to be strong!"

PSALM 62:1-2 "God, the one and only – I'll wait as long as he says. Everything I need comes from him, so why not? He's solid rock under my feet, breathing room for my soul, an impregnable castle: I'm set for life."

I heard a rumbling in the sky coming from behind me. I got S...c...a...r...e...d!!!!! I reached behind for my slingshot. Then I heard a big thundering ROAR and the lightening lit up the whole sky. I had to get home, but I stopped in sudden fear. My legs would no longer peddle. What was that Bible verse? What was it that made me stand strong like David? "God," I cried out, "I need You!"

PSALM 34:4 "GOD met me more than halfway, he freed me from my anxious fears."

I looked down at my slingshot, felt a strength rise within me. I reached towards the ground for a pebble on the sidewalk. I put it in my slingshot and shouted from the deepest part of my heart, "I am strong and courageous. I will not be terrified, for the Lord, my God, is with me!"

I released the stone, flying into the air.

Wow! I think I feel better, a little stronger, less fearful.

JOSHUA 1:7 "Haven't I commanded you? Strength! Courage! Don't be timid; don't get discouraged. GOD, your God, is with you every step you take."

I was ready to get back on my bike. I grabbed one more pebble before jumping back on.

I put the pebble in the sling, turned around and took aim. I declared, "I do not have a spirit of fear, but of power, love and a sound mind!" I felt the power of the words as I shot the pebble from the sling. POW. The pebble took off just like the words springing from my heart.

I put my feet on the peddles and peddled so fast I thought my legs were on fire. But I wasn't afraid! My insides weren't trying to rip apart! I could peddle my bike! I was now peddling fast not from fear but because I knew I should get inside before the storm came.

Shooting fear with God's Word really did make me feel strong and courageous.

JEREMIAH 1:7-8 "GOD told me, "Don't say, 'I'm only a boy.' I'll tell you where to go and you'll go there. I'll tell you what to say and you'll say it. Don't be afraid of a soul. I'll be right there, looking after you."

I saw my mom waving from the front door. "I was getting ready to come look for you," my mom shouted.

"It's okay, Mom," I yelled back as I drove up the driveway to the garage door that was open and waiting for me to ride my bike into.

PSALM 27:1 "Light, space, zest—that's GOD. So, with him on my side I'm fearless, afraid of no one and nothing."

My mom came running into the garage from the house with a towel and her arms opened wide. I ran into them laughing and crying because I wasn't afraid anymore. I understood the power of God's Word. His Word gave me strength to battle my fear.

Now I can say with confidence...

David trusted His God when he felt afraid, SO DO I.

David is brave and So Am I......